Billy Boy

I0895410

Rosemary Jenkinson

BILLY BOY

ARLEN
HOUSE

Billy Boy

is published in 2022 by
ARLEN HOUSE
42 Grange Abbey Road
Baldoyle
Dublin D13 A0F3
Ireland
Email: arlenhouse@gmail.com
arlenhouse.ie

ISBN 978–1–85132–283–1, paperback

International distribution
SYRACUSE UNIVERSITY PRESS
621 Skytop Road, Suite 110
Syracuse
New York 13244–5290
USA
Email: supress@syr.edu
www.syracuseuniversitypress.syr.edu

© Rosemary Jenkinson, 2022

The moral right of the author has been asserted

Typesetting by Arlen House

Cover images: John Travers as Billy Boy
by Ross Reaney (front cover) and Matt Faris (back cover)
are reproduced courtesy of the photographers

Internal photographs are by Ross Reaney and Matt Faris

arts council of Northern Ireland

LOTTERY FUNDED

CONTENTS

Introduction

I could say that the genesis of *Billy Boy* was the moment I approached Rachel Kennedy of EastSide Arts in autumn 2019 to write a play on bonfire culture, but that wouldn't be quite accurate. Prior to that, I'd had a conversation with Maurice Kinkead of EastSide Partnership about the contemporary side of East Belfast where some of the new generation, rather than fetishizing the Dutch King William of Orange, are likely to have partners from Holland, or indeed any country. So much art is born out of chance exchanges.

The idea behind the play was to defy the simplistically negative depictions of East Belfast in the media. I wanted to shine a light on the Protestant/loyalist community that surrounds me – not in any sugar-coated hagiography I should add, but with all its flaws and challenges. The bonfires I was highlighting are the architectural behemoths that burst into your eyeline every summer. They seem to be almost vying with the Harland & Wolff cranes that tower over the landscape. 'We are here and we are not leaving this land,' the bonfires proclaim on one level; on another, they are part of a joyous cultural festival with no agenda whatsoever.

And so, the production was scheduled for August 2020, but that was before the plague swept in and plans were abandoned. In early 2021, EastSide Arts arranged zoom sessions for me and director Matt Faris with teenage bonfire builders from community groups. I'd much rather have strolled down to a bonfire site with a carry-out as I did for my research for *The Bonefire*, my very first play produced by Rough Magic, but the times they had a-changed. Parties had stopped and the only thing we were putting down our throats and sticking up our nostrils was a testing stick! Still, I learnt a great deal from the zoom sessions such as how bonfire sites were being systematically removed by city councils as part of the ongoing Catholic/Protestant culture wars.

A film version of *Billy Boy* was screened in June 2021 and, gloriously, the theatre production took place in August as part of EastSide Arts Festival. Theatre was back in its raw unfettered essence. With bated breath, I watched John Travers brilliantly burn up the stage and light up my words with all the inner fire of a true East Belfast boy.

– May 2022

Performance Rights

For permission to perform this play, contact Rosemary Jenkinson, c/o The Lyric Theatre, Belfast.

Performance History

Billy Boy was first performed at the Strand Arts Centre as part of the EastSide Arts Festival on 7 August 2021 with the following cast and creatives:

Writer: Rosemary Jenkinson
Director: Matt Faris
Actor: John Travers
Stage Manager: Seána Green
Set and Costume Designer: Tracey Lindsay
Sound designer: Marty Byrne
Community Liaison: Aimee Consiglia Conway
Line Producer: Stephen Beggs
Producer: Rachel Kennedy for EastSide Arts

Billy Boy

Characters

Aaron Orr, twenty, plays all parts including King William III

Setting

An East Belfast bonfire
time period 1690–2021

KING WILLIAM III: So we have it. The Boyne. The wooden ford. Our scouts say the water's deep after yesterday's biblical flood. Over there, you can see the smoke from their camp, dark wreaths in the dawn. The French shouting out, mocking us across the river. The House of Orange will fight when the orange sun rises. *(Grabs his own shoulder in pain).* Aagh. It's a graze from yesterday's cannon shot, but what did they make that gunpowder from, magic druid blood? At least my life was spared.

By grace of God we will win. The Enniskilleners, the Derry skirmishers are all on my side. My Dutch Blue are strong, the Huguenots, the Germans, the best of Europe united. Can't trust the English mercenaries though. I'm King of England and I still can't trust them.

To think, today my blood will fight against me. Two opposing hills. James, my uncle and my father-in-law, twice bound to me in blood ...

The low beat of a drum.

I'll try to spare him if I can. The sky is lightening. The mist is creeping along the Boyne with a cold knife in its teeth. The Scots-Irish tell me it's fairy breath, and to set the ambush. The land blesses us!

Rush of drums, then stops.

AARON: Here's me. Hot sunny Belfast, tenth of July, the reek of melting tar, drips of ice cream splattered like paint bombs, and it's a blister, a glister of a day, and I'm chilling on the street, sunnies on, sat back in me director's cut chair, the light licking me locks. Everyone and their granny is out, oul lad next door is that leathered, weathered from the sun, he looks like a bog body. Wee kids collecting cash in buckets like they're at the beach, couple of lads are putting some bunting up, fella on the ladder swaying like he's a circus act on stilts, but I'm blissed out under the beams, beaming to the seams when –

Beep beep. *(Looks down at his phone).* Talks have broken down. Health and safety! Fuck me, our bonefire builders are expert, we don't just throw it up. Light it evenly, it collapses in the middle. Won't fall anywhere near the houses. Here, the only injury you can cop from our boney is from standing on a nail!

Bumpety-bump-bump tunes banging out a wee hot hatch and it's Deano in the moonbeam mobile.

Here, Aaron, it's kicking off! shouts Deano, skidding to a stop. I hoof it over, jumps in and we're offski, speeding like a maniac, him so fast I'm like this with me fingernails in the dashboard.

See? he says, banging the brakes.

Ten meat wagons and six white contractor vans. Squad of ninjas lined up, all batons and riot shields. Two wee kids on top of the bonefire flipping them the finger. Already a big crowd's gathering. I spot a few wee hoods hiding in an entry with a crate of petrol bombs, but Davey Weir walks over, shoulders rolling like a pitbull, won't let them use them unless the baggie blues move in and drag the kids off the boney. Contractor fellas in their balaclavas – just who *are* the paramilitaries round here, like? Tell me that.

Fuck away off, the wee kids shout down, fair fucks to them, like.

The big gob of the JCB slowly opens – *kggkkkrre* – like it's longing to swallow them up. The council won't be happy till they've removed every last bonefire from our city. Aye, nice the way the peelers re-enact the siege of Londonderry every year, laying siege to our boneys.

Get stuck into them! Deano shouts, burning fierce like the sun.

Settle yourself, growls Davey Weir.

Hey, that's my wee lad up there! gulders Bethany, barging through lines of peelers who are caught napping, and she and her mates are running through them like the Charge of the Light Brigade. They lock arms round the bonefire. What a manoeuvre and everyone cheers!

The peeler with a loudhailer, Jesus, he's as bad as them bible bashers on the street telling us we're going to hell.

You are trespassing on council land. If you don't leave now, you will be arrested.

But Bethany won't budge. A Mexican standoff as the peelers weigh up whether to weigh in but the press rock up, and the peelers realise they're up against women and kids, which is not so hot on the PR side. Phones are pinging, the crowd's growing, so the contractors, heads baking like a spud in their black ballies, get inside their white vans and drive off and the peelers slink off too.

Yes! We won! shouts Davey Weir. Sash before cash! The East 1 – City Council 0! Yeoh!

Trouble is they'll be back for the rematch. Even if they don't get you for health and safety, all it takes is one complaint from a virtue signaler saying they don't like the eyesore. Know why folk really don't like our bonefire? Cos it's wild, lawless in a world gone mad with rules and regs. Like, are we going to apply for planning permission? No chance.

Sure the council threw us off our last spot, so we had to come here. You know the real laugh of it? The council was fed up cleaning up every wee boney at the end of the street, so it was them who said, 'Go you and build one big bonfire for the whole district.' And now they're yapping about them being too big. But they started it!

Aye, the council give you three grand if you light one of their skittery wee beacons, but who wants that? Freedom is everything. You think we're filling in their dopey oul forms? Even if they give you the cash, they can take most of it back if they see a tyre or a flag or it's untidy or too high. Know what it is? Compromise = sell-out.

Anyway, we'll have to do an all-nighter to guard it. The contractors can hit you any time, from dusk till dawn. You gotta be primed, locked and loaded to keep them out.

I'll get a forty bag of green to keep me up, says Jamesie.

I'll get a wrap of speed, says Dean.

Fuck sake, it's like being with the chemical brothers. I don't even do drugs, but the fucking dealers hang round our boney like flies – they don't care if it's the Twelfth or St Paddy's, they'd fleece you blind whatever, but I stick forty quid into the kitty for the schwall because it's the eleventh tomorrow and we might as well start partying and do a double-nighter. I whip into the offies and get us a boatload of Bud and some cider on the side. Then Deano drops us home.

Me ma fixes me a dirty big feed of a fry for my tea, a real gutbuster to get me through the night.

Now, don't be getting into trouble tonight, will you, son.

Course I won't, I never do.

Huh, she says, huh. I *know* you. Sure you're on your last warning.

Fair enough, the peelers have called round a few times. The older ones once told us there were tyres waiting at a tyre shop, so over we went and got them. We didn't know we were stroking them, did we? You have to watch the older ones. Sketchy as fuck – they want to get you a criminal rec so you join their ranks.

At ten I dander down to the boney. And look, the moon is up and it's orange from the glow of the city lights, shining down on us, an orange moon, not an Orangeman, gettit? And I'm in great form, slapping the 'to let' boards as I pass, high-five! 'Copter hovering up above, buzzing like an angry bee. Eye in the sky eyeing us good style – know how much it costs to put it up there? Ten grand a day, like!

Alright, bros?

Deano and Jamesie are there already with the C/O.

Here, Aaron, get this down ye!

Deano passes us a bottle.

Cheers, mate.

And I'm about to neck it when I see it's got a cloth in it. It's a petrol bomb!

Get it away to fuck, but Deano's having a knicker fit laughing, says the teenagers have stashed petrol bombs between the pallets just in case the peelers kick off tonight. I pile into the Bud. Been saving up for the Twelfth and haven't been out in two weeks. My body feels like it's under house arrest!

Glug-glug-a-glug-glug – aahhh ...

Bod fliuch, béal fliuch agus bás in Ulster!

What the fuck?

Jamesie's taking Irish lessons down the Skainos and he's always showing off, slabbering Gael talk like we're in the Gaeltacht, pretending he's saying something profound.

Course I don't mind. I'm not bigoted. As long as he doesn't start shouting *Tiocfaidh ár Lá* it's grand.

More pallets are dropped off – class! Our boney's forty foot and flying! We bate everywhere last year. We're repping the whole of the East!

The young girls rock up with some wood. Jamesie's the babemeister, the hot stuff of us.

Go on, Jamesie, speak that Gaelic to us, would you? says one of the girls, fulla fake tan, Kerry Leigh or Dairy Lea, as Deano calls her.

What's your name, a girl asks us.

Ach, don't bother with Aaron, he doesn't like girls, says Dairy Lea.

Hey, it's me cousin that's gay, not me. Jesus, he came out last year and the way my aunt goes on it's like she's reared a child prodigy. You'd think being gay was a fucking achievement these days like 10 GCSEs, something for the CV, like.

Brrr, getting chilly out here. That coul you could hang beef, so Deano lights a fire.

Go on there, Bear Grylls, cackles Dairy Lea.

Here, says Deano, let's get on the schniff to make us last till morning.

I haven't done drugs in years, but I'm getting right and wrecked on the beer, and Deano's holding the back of his hand out with a wee eyebrow of speed on it, and I know I shouldn't, but I need a wee livener, so ...

Sccchniiiifff ...

What? Me sinuses have just hit the back of my head, but result, I'm bang awake. I feel like a vampire that's just mainlined a crack addict's arm. Even worse I've probably snorted Dean's DNA out his skin. I'm in real trouble now, I'll turn into a right mooncat.

Some of the youngbloods are down at the wall, spraying a message – 'Attack Loyalism at Your Own Risk'. Amateurs – big drips running down the concrete, so down I bounce, grab one of the spray cans and show them how it's done.

Just then, one of the peeler vans slides round and –

Scatter-match! Run like fuck!

We belt down an entry, hop over a yard wall and into some youngblood's house. Then I nip out all on my ownio, right back to the boney-o.

Here, says Deano, you'll be scooped for that, you dunderhead, you blunderhead, you didn't even have your scarf across your face.

And he's right for it's one of those peeler vans with a camera on the top, tout's charter down its side – Crimestoppers Anonymous on such and such. Can't believe I've been such a dick.

Here, neck another Bud and forget about it.

Alright for you, Deano, it's my hoop on the line here. I get a record, how'll I get a job?

Deano's a Glider driver and we rip the piss pure off him. Him and his big bendy purple thing. Like, I had a job in youth work, but it stopped a month ago, so now I'm on me hole on the rock'n'roll.

Never mind. Dip down for a beer, but they're gone. Deano and Jamesie are human skips when it comes to the schwall.

Have a wee swally of my whiskey, sure says Dairy Lea. Nicked it out the house.

I never touch whiskey. Water of Life, they call it. Water of Strife, I call it. Me da used to go buckmad on it, had to go to the door store after taking it as he'd kicked half the doors in. But, what the hell, a wee dose won't hurt, will it?

A wee swall and another. Ah, it's nice and warming. Flames flickering, drizzle falling and we don't even feel it. See fire? You need it when you've the shittiest climate in the world. Fire brings you closer to everyone. I could almost fall for Dairy Lea. Well, almost. Me eyes start to close.

Have just realised I need the speed to counteract the whiskey. It's a vicious circle.

Chill, it's nature's cycle, says Jamesie, handing me a joint.

No way, bro, the only joint I take is for my Sunday dinner, the only hash I take is a hash brown, the only blow I like is a blow job.

Aye, but the grass is always greener on the other side. *Is glas iad na cnoc i bhfad uainn.*

Wow, goes Dairy Lea. I love you speaking that Gaelic.

A car flies round. Slows down to look at our boney and mebbie they've come to burn it down, so Deano grabs an unopened can of cider and slam –

Yeohhhh – buries it right in the passenger door, and off they rev, tyres squealing like a pig in an abattoir.

And the peeler van wheels round again and I can see the camera on top and I'm that feared I'm going to be done I pull up my scarf, flip up my hood and clip my way over.

N-o-o-o, shouts Jamesie behind me, but the blood is up and I'm racing towards it now and I'm dancing round the van like Conor McGregabollix, eyeing that camera like a demon and I do a spinning high-kick, leaping into the air like a suspended samurai ...

Haaiiiiiii ...

No I don't, for that's just in movies. Me, I jump up and punch it one, a right welter-belter.

Aaow! My hand!

But at least the camera's looking down now and can't spy on us any more. Peeler van bumps to a halt as they think of hurtling out after me, but I'm gone again up the entry, flying like fuck and this time I go home, and the sky's already lightening at four by the time I headbutt the pillow and I feel bad for abandoning the night watch but me comrades, Deano and Jamesie, will make it through.

The next morning, I am hanging like a bat. Ah, ah, ah, it's like I'm a digger lifting a load up, it's like the contents of me head could fall out at any minute. Pop down to the kitchen cause we have a serious rehydration situation on the go.

That clear white reservoir screeching out the tap – eeeeek. Shut up! Me head's hammering!

Knock it back. Gul-gul-a-gul-gul-gul.

It all floods back to me. Oh God, I am scundered a hundred. Check out the local news. Our bonefire's still there, but ...

'Police are looking for a man of about twenty, athletic build, for causing criminal damage to one of their vehicles last night.'

Only raking you. There's nothing about me. But there is a piece about the sinister graffiti on the wall. What if the peelers got me on camera, what if they identify me? They love to scoop loyalists. PSNI – stands for Politically Sensitive to Nationalist Interests. And there's worse ...

'This morning, the police discovered petrol bombs hidden within in the controversial bonfire.'

Oh no-o-o ... me fingerprints were all over it. Me arse is squirming like a squirrel's nose. I have the Gary Glitters, the skitters alright.

Toilet, quick shower, pull the strides on, flick at the hair, crack open the paracetamol, then think no, go and get some real medicine. No, not the doc's, like, off for a swiftie to the pub to get a cure.

Outside, the sun's splitting the trees. The roses, the honeysuckle, the green grass going gold in the sun – flowers wilting but the rays are reviving me.

Walk down past the boney, and it's mad, there's even this van with a big satellite dish waiting to see if the contractors come back for round two, ding-ding. Some wee dweeb of a reporter is asking what folk think of the council's ruling, but everyone's ignoring him and there's a kids' street party, all these bouncy castles sprouting up like mushrooms.

The reporter's face is tripping him without his big scoop.

Here, I call out, how about a story on the community coming together?

Who wants that? he says sourly. We don't do good news stories on loyalists.

Unbelievable. I'm just passing the Disco Dome and there's some sort of stir inside, like a riot going on, aye, the dome is rocking with people off their domes.

Yeoh! Let's go!

I recognise that voice. The Disco Dome Man leaps into the Dome and hauls out Deano and Jamesie, still full as a gipsy's tit from last night.

This is for the kids, you mentalists! Dome Man shouts after them.

Relax the keks, goes Deano, then spots me. Oh, look, it's the wee sly-off himself!

Here, wait, goes Jamesie, pointing to the TV camera. Go and kill it, Aaron, bate the bollocks out of it.

Yeah, yeah, very funny.

Uh-oh. Davey Weir's outside the pub and us three sneaky past when ... Davey hooks me by the hoodie and I'm caught like a flapping fish.

Here, you, what about them petrol bombs last night?

Face on him like a bulldog licking the piss off jaggy nettles.

It wasn't us, says Deano. Was the young ones planked them.

And what about that peeler van?

Wasn't us, Davey.

Davey Weir looks at us suspicious, then drops it, drops *me*.

Aye, well, fair play for manning the boney, lads. Much appreciated.

Whew, and on we go into the pub. There's a live band playing eighties hits. Fuck me, the musicians are nearly as old as the music!

So, what are you having, lads, says Deano, apart from a good afternoon? A wee whiskey?

Thought of it near makes me boke my ring up.

Pints all round then, goes Deano.

I tell Jamesie I need to get out of Belfast in case the peelers scoop me.

Ach, you'll be fine, he says. A problem ignored is a problem solved.

But what if I'm not fine? Are there no jobs at that club in Corfu?

In three days' time, Jamesie's off to work as a bartender in Corfu. Sun, sea, sand, sex and sambuca, that'll do me. I get me phone out, check it out but typical, flights cost a mint if you're skint.

Deano's got his own probs cause he's due a drug test when he goes back to the Glider in two days and he's scarfed too much speed.

Flush it out with water and milk thistle, advises Bethany, the barwoman, all profesh.

I remember last Twelfth he had a piss test. That morning, he got his sister to pish into a condom, then wrapped it round his balls. As soon as his boss sent him into the bogs, he poured it into a cup, sorted! The only problem, the results came back and they told him he was clear in every way, but for one very strange thing – it seemed he was fucking pregnant!

See how much trouble the Prodfest gets us into? Sure my sister works for the DVA, her office is full of folk hating the Twelfth, so she has to let on she's in Donegal for the week.

We bounce out after our pints, feeling sound as a pound.

At least our boney's safe with the press camped there and the kiddiwinks out in full force. The council would look like the baddies if they touched it.

You're not welcome here, Davey Weir's telling an American cameraman. Last time the Americans rocked up, they asked a teenage girl why she celebrated the boney and she said, 'I don't know. Jesus's birthday?'

They were laughing at her all over the world but how was it her fault? Sure we're taught British history at school when we should be taught Irish history.

Before we know it, Jamesie's strutting over to a TV crew like he's Timothée Chalamet.

So here's the craic. Three years ago we let a bonefire go in exchange for the council promising not to get rid of any more boneys, but now there's a newly-elected council going, 'It wasn't us who promised you, was it?' When's it gonna end? They keep driving us off the land – wait, I was crinkling me eyes there in the sun, could you just fillum that again ... me left side's me good side ... me name ...? Jamie Bryson.

Fuck sake, it's not an audition, Jamesie, we say, pulling him away. You gotta be careful. If you end up on TV or Twitter, you can be branded for life, you can lose your job for it.

Beat of the Lambeg accompanied by flutes.

And they're off. Our band's walking down the road.

The Lambegger's big as a bull, his back arched, he's like Atlas lifting the stone, veins pumping out his neck, drum up on his belly, bating the guts out of it, giving it rice.

Louder and louder it beats in your chest, you need to be drunk to bear it, bangs through your body and brains, the joy of it, the Duke of Schomberg's call to battle.

The sticks pounding and vibrating on the pure white of the taut goatskin, dimpling, quivering ...

It's times like this I love this place and then I remember last night's graffiti and the peeler van – no, Aaron, ignore it. But I can't.

Wish I hadn't splashed the cash on booze either. At least I have the last of me cash in my account. I google Cheap Flights. And I'm thinking somewhere cool, like, not the arsehole of nowhere. Amsterdam from £19.99 flashes up, lastminute.com, and I'm thinking it's just clickbait and it'll be triple when I try to buy, but there are still flights for £19.99 tomorrow morning ...

Here, let's get a kitty sorted for tonight, goes Deano.

And I'm thinking, Amsterdam's cool – Amstel beer's from Amsterdam – and I press book before it's too late. And just like that I'm going, I'm outta here. Deano's gob hits the ground.

Here, bet you'll be back in a week. You'll be hiding from the peelers just like whatsername, Anne Frank under the floorboards!

I head home to pack. The ma is gobsmacked.

You're going *where*?

Amsterdam.

You're in trouble, aren't you? You're being run out of town, that's it.

No, I'm just leaving this country for better opportunities.

Sure there's Brexit, they won't like us over there. No, you're in trouble. Remember, I *know* you.

Nothing like the good oul Ulster ma for support.

Look, ok ... I'm not perfect. The reason I left me cross-community youth work was because some wee lad called a girl a stupid wee Orangie. See, the Shinner ones are plugged into their history and think we're dense, but we just haven't been trained to debate like them. Aye, I may have twatted him but it was only a wee dunt, not a fully-fledged schmack. If it was out in the street, like, I'd have kicked the wee cunt's stoners in, but I know, I know I'm meant to be all mature and adulty now and to deal with sectarian slurs in a responsible, verbal manner, my fault, like, hands up to that – and besides, how is Orangie an insult, sure my culture's Orange – anyway, I resigned.

Sure son how'll you fit in with themmuns speaking foreign over there?

What? You'd think I'd never met anyone from another country. Sure half the street's Polish. And isn't it bad enough with Jamesie and his Irish.

Grumbling, she helps pack my case, devises a special going-away dinner.

That night I walk down to the boney. All around, the youngbloods are putting the boards up on the windies to protect them. Others are tying election posters of a Shinner and an Alliancer onto the pallets. The media are snapping it, but come on to fuck, these politicians are trying to stop our bonefires, so what do they expect? The tradition of burning political effigies goes all the way back to Guy Fawkes. Like, d'you want us to get the marshmallows and roast chestnuts out – jog on, like! A tricolour flying from the top too. If the Shinners are going to hang you, you might as well get hung for the whole heap, eh?

And it's time! And I feel it – shiver-rivers down my spine.

Biggest boney in the East, everyone's shouting. Wee Roma boy is banging on a red, white and blue drum with two biros The Scotsies are cheering, DJ's on the decks, rave anthems bouncing out, heard one, heard em both.

Here, have one for the road, mate, says Dean, passing us a beer.

Aye, go on then, one for the flightpath, eh, Deano?

The rave stops and the DJ plays the tune from *Braveheart*.

And you feel the stir in here, something epic, as the boney collectors march up with their torches – it's not exactly an Olympic torch, just a broom handle with a cloth, but it does the biz. Davey Weir douses them in petrol and sparks them up. There's more petrol on our boney than a fucking Maxol station! Over they troop to the boney and climb up the tiers and cheer on the top, and *yeeoohh*, she's sparkers, flames flying. Near roasts your eyeballs off, the heat'd last you to Christmas.

We can't stop staring at it, pulls us into its glow, it's mesmerizing, it's primal, black pallets falling into the bright orange. And the rave's back on and the youngbloods are pumping the air, fisting the sky. Everyone lit to the boards and half won't even make it to the Twelfth – here, lads, it's about the battle, not the bottle, but sure it's cool to go wild.

A wee girl dressed in pink gives it the oul technicolour yawn, pukes up a load of pink over my feet.

Not like me to skin out of a party, but I might miss me flight if I don't. I say goodbye to Deano and Jamesie who are that juiced they're on mumble-mode, give them the knuckle-shuffle, then go.

I'm down the road when I hear steps beating behind me and – wow, it's Jamesie hugging me and I'll miss the bones of you, man, he tells me and I say, me too, and I'm tearing up, so I turn away and go.

Slán go fóill, a chara, his call comes after me, trailing into the air which is almost white. The whole city's bathed in wreaths of smoke, Belfast looks like it's already fading away from me, as pale as a memory.

The taxi comes at five. And the birds are all out singing for me.

Where you off? goes the driver, chucking me case in the boot. Anywhere good?

Amsterdam. (Burst of pride in me chest even though he's probably thinking I'm after the weed and the prozzies).

Great, going for long?

Dunno. Just gonna scope it out and see. (How cool am I? Just like Louis fucking Theroux).

Pass by the boney, the ground's all black charcoal, grey ash and smoking, smouldering embers just like after a Native American powwow. Here, it takes three months to build and only three hours to burn! That's life, isn't it? Round it, all the empty bottles, dope bags scuttling along in the breeze, burger boxes impaled on the church railings ...

A right state, eh? tuts the driver.

Sinn Féin or Alliance Party. You can tell by the tone.

Well, ok, so it's not as pretty here as Cyprus Avenue.

Aye, no trees, but a dirty pile of wood at the end of your street, he sniggers, the hate hanging out of him.

Is this what peace brought? Before, people used to hide their true feelings cause they were scared of being splatted for it, but now they crow all over us, gloat away.

Thank God I'm outta here. Over and out.

Lights out. The busy traffic, honks of horns in Amsterdam.

Lights up, as the sun comes up.

August, the heat of the traffic. You'd think the canals would cool the air, but they don't. The first few days I kipped in a cheap hostel for fifteen quid a night. Then asked around for jobs. These Polish lads said they were picking strawberries, and could score us a lift to the farm if I wanted. Wanted? I didn't have a wing, down to me last few euro. Shoulda seen the queue of us the next morning. Fake name, fake social security number and off out to the field, one giant furrow apiece. On your marks, set, go and everyone else is belting up their lane, you'd think they were in the Olympics, arms flying like windmills. I was near a mile behind the Poles, scrabbling along like a badger digging out worms when they taught me the trick, fill the bottom of the box with unripe strawbs, then fill the top with the best, so the supervisor thinks you're only picking the finest. So, I started hoovering them up, flinging them into the boxes and it wasn't bad, a bit backbreaking crawling around like a ba-ba under the big baby blue of the sky, but the perk is you're out in the sun, shirt off, muscles out, tanned to the gills, brown from the sun and the soil.

Then Friday, flash the cash in the pubs and clubs. I roll with the Poles, only they're saving their readies. Just as well their culture is to drink vodka neat – saves you on the mixer, amn't I right?

Then Monday morning, back to Strawberry Fields Forever. Hard graft, but at least I don't have to sit in me undies in an Amsterdam street window. Though I reckon I'd score a wee juke or two with me tan, slicked up with suncream. Sometimes I'm lonely, like, but, here's the thing, it's only being lonely that you ever get to think.

Lucky enough, the Dutch are great at English and even their own words sound sort of like English – *excuseer, dank ye*. It's no worse than listening to pissed-up punters in the pub.

One Saturday I'm on the tram back from the Red Light District and the Rembrandt House Museum – see, I like a bit of culture with me sex tourism, mix it up, like. And this tram is rammers, like, hiving, and we're all jammed up, squidged against the windies, and my hands are rammed against me and suddenly I feel me left hand slammed up between a woman's legs and oh fuck, I try to move my hand to wriggle it away, but it makes it even worse, it's like I'm fingering her now, and Jesus fuck, there's this girl staring at me five inches away and 'sorry' I mumble.

What? she says.

Sorry.

And she smiles, not understanding, and suddenly I realise it's not her I'm feeling, it must be the granny next to her, yeaaccch! The sweat is lashing off us, what if the granny calls me out, accuses me, but it's like we're all slapped into each other in that game, whatyoucallit, Twister. And, thank fuck, the doors whoosh open at the next stop and me hand, it's suddenly released from the oul doll and whew, that coulda been me, like, on the sex offender's register, like, pervert alert just cause of a tram jam.

And the girl is still next to me, smiling at my relief.

Crazy, isn't it? she says.

Aye, near as wild as our Glider.

What?

She says 'what' a lot. That's cause her English, like most of the Dutch, is better than mine. Her name's Yolanda and she has hair goldier than Van Gogh's *Sunflowers* and wow.

I blow off the Poles (not literally, like) and meet her that night. She takes us to a coffee shop and I'm thinking shite, I'm jittery enough as it is without coffee, I need a drink to relax me, like, I can't do a date sober, fuck me, I've hardly ever had sex sober.

This big menu comes. You'd think we were in this posh-nosh restaurant. I'll have the scallops in *beurre de garlique, garçon*.

But it's all *haute cuisine de cannabis* and she orders us some superskunk space cake.

Look, I don't do dope, I fess up, it melts my head.

Ok, I'll get you the White Widow Space Cake. I'll break you in slowly.

And I'm feeling like a right wimpy wussballs. And I eat some and it's buzzy and a trippy wee treat and we're laughing away and I'm telling her about King Billy and the bonefire ...

I'm a Catholic, you know.

That's grand, I say. I'm only sectarian in Belfast, and not even much then.

One thing I know about our King William is he liked young men. They say he promoted them in his court to have sex with them.

Fair play. There's this song, Good King Billy Had a Ten-Foot Willy, so he had to put it somewhere. Besides, my cousin's gay. He's that out the closet he's nearly in Narnia.

What? she says.

Nothing.

Are you single? she says.

Aye.

Well, let's be single together then.

I didn't make it back to the fields for two days ... Well, I'd like to say we were in bed the whole time but it was me alone on her sofa, head still pasted from the space cake, whitied out to the bollocks, didn't know where I was.

You'll get used to it, she says.

Aye, I'll apply my Protestant drink ethic to it. I'll get there alright, but, here, no wonder Van Gogh chopped his ear off – Van Gone more like, off his melter on the superskunk.

It's mad but Yolanda and me, we've nothing in common. She's a real eco-warrior, she's studying environmental science, aye, she's a clever clogs alright. Clogs, Dutch, gettit? Yaps at me for not recycling me Amstel bottles, cycles round the town. Who'd have thought I'd end up with Greta fucking Thunberg!

Even when I was telling her about our history, filling her in on the plantation, she thought I was talking about planting trees! Like, of course I agree the earth's important and all, but see politics? It's like a pair of new shoes. People are all, what do I look good in, what do I sound good saying?

But she's hot for my body all sweat and strawberry-stained from the fields, these warm nights, her body slap-slap-slapping against mine like the whap of a sweaty boxing glove on skin. Only problem is, the end of August comes, all misty and the strawberries shrivel up.

Dunno what to do. Yolanda wants me to stay. I can't scrounge off a student, like. When it comes to drinks I want to go Dutch – ha! I start a job in a light bulb factory, but it's not what I want to do with me life. Makes me so tired, I'm out like a bulb.

The lights go out, then come back on.

Then, something happens.

Lights flicker on and off like a bad electrical connection.

Covid and I'm furloughed. Would have headed home to see the team and the fam in the summer, but the only boney allowed is a firepit in their garden. I keep remembering all the summers when I was a wee kid, collecting pallets in a trolley – here, our hut was better built than half the social housing these days – and the sleepovers and how it was like camping, looking up at the starry dome of the sky, and my first ever kiss ... not that it was all bliss. The older ones would tell you another bonefire had nicked our wood and get you to raid theirs ... but apart from that, it was magic.

In Amsterdam, life goes slow, sitting in with Yolanda night after night. Go back to packing light bulbs – at least I can say I'm bringing a bit of brightness into people's lives.

In July, I'm just thinking of Belfast when – a call from me ma.

Jamesie. Gone into a spiral since Covid began, going boogaloo, smoking too much, shutting himself in his room and ...

Pack the bags quick. Yolanda comes too as she wants to meet everyone.

Why don't you bring back something nice from Amsterdam for your friends?

What like, superskunk? It's not legal. I'd have to put it in a condom and stick it up me arse. I can just see me checking into KLM.

How many items of luggage are you checking in, sir?

Two – one in the hold and one up the hole, thanks.

Better not. Buy the ma some Delft instead.

We get a flight to Dublin Airport on a wee puddle-jumper. Yolanda feels all guilty flying cause it's not environmental but I say, enjoy it, sure you could be a refugee in a dinghy paddling across the channel. Then a bus up to Belfast. At the border, there's a big sign 'Welcome to Northern Ireland', only the Northern's graffitied out and replaced by 'One'. Welcome to One Ireland. Fuck aff. Oops, think I might have said that out loud.

What? goes Yolanda.

Nothing, baby, just crossing the border. Now, put your clock back thirty years – only raking your bacon.

There's this massive rainbow up ahead and the bus rides straight for it, like we're going through a glorious gateway.

Bit worried now in case Deano comes out with one of his lines about Yolanda like, 'She's so ugly the tide wouldn't take her out.' Like, not that she's ugly in any way. She's stunning but just doesn't bother with orange makeup. She's a feminist but me mates are hardly 'woke'. Fuck me, they're barely awake!

We get in the taxi and go to the East.

It's mad, I'm looking at everything like it's a new country. The flags jigging in the wind like the lamp posts are trying to shake them off.

What is this? Buy a flag, get one free day? scoffs the taxi driver.

No guessing which religion he's from, eh? But I'm chill. Whatevs, I say.

Is today a festival? asks Yolanda.

Every day is a festival here, Yolanda. See the fence, that's the interface.

All these colours and murals, she says. Why do you have to prove who you are? Don't you know who you are?

(AARON *shrugs).* In this country, if you don't prove it, you lose it.

The ma hugs us like she hasn't seen us in years. And literally, she hasn't.

Don't know how you can stick him, Yolanda. Only raking you, wee pet, wee dote!

Jesus, Ma, cringe city.

Ach, Yolanda's lovely, she whispers to me in the kitchen.

Doesn't bat an eyelid when she hears she's Catholic. Ten years ago, my sister brought a guy home she introduced as Mal. The ma thought he was Malcolm – no one had the nerve back then to tell her he was Malachy.

I show Yolanda the bonefire. She thinks it's mega, never seen anything like it in her life. It's smaller this year cause we've given wood to the Shankill after their boney got burnt down.

Deano bounces up. Me bro! And the oul familiar slagging.

Look at the state of ye, he goes. More spud than stud. What are you doing with him, Yolanda? He's that ugly his ma fed him with a cattypult. That ugly even the tide wouldn't take him out! Here, you must be switched on to work at a bulb factory. Switched on, eh?

Balloon.

He's going steady with Dairy Lea. Her fake tan is even more orange than before. Sure she's as orange now as the rind on a Dutch Gouda. Yolanda's so different, like. Natural. Even has her own eyebrows.

Deano still drives the Glider, bringing our teenagers to Falls Park, their teenagers to our boney. Things have changed in two years alright, but we're still being sold down the river – or in this case, the sea.

And it's Jamesie! You're the colour of milk, you'd think it was winter.

Cad é an dóigh, a chara.

Give him a hug, hope you're ok, bro.

But look, Aaron.

Yolanda spots a mattress chucked in the hollow. Must have been the wee kids turfed it in, the hallions, it all goes to rack and ruin without us.

Look at all the broken glass, says Yolanda, and it's from the wee kids, wee scrotes, wee skiprats – they should be playing spin the bottle, not smash the bottle! Now I'm back, I see I'm going to have to run me own bonfire management scheme! Jesus, if Yolanda knew I used to plank tyres in the boney, she'd go buckmad. Ten years ago it was more toxic than a nuclear plant! There are some tyres sitting at the side, but we can't stop the flytippers – we're just not putting them on our boney, no way. But Sinn Féin? They're hiding sectarianism behind environmentalism. What about all your fucking bombs in the past? You weren't thinking about the environment then, were you?

Tobacco pouches skittering round the road, Kapake strips, crisp packets, everything bad for you and Yolanda's making a show of herself picking things up. But she's right, like, you shouldn't shite in your own nest. And it's mad, cause most people's gaffs are wee clean palaces, so, lads, how did we lose the run of our streets?

Baile an Chacamair, says Jamesie. Ballyhackamore – did you know that means Town of the Big Shit? Sure East Belfast's not meant to be clean.

I take Jamesie to one side. Says he's County Down some days, but he's seeing the head doctor and working things through. Getting his act together.

Thank God, mate.

He tells us the latest. Another boney gone in the East. The Housing Exec's building more playgrounds just to get rid of our sites.

And this year, the council's playing the health and safety card again and has ruled for the bonefire's removal. Trailed through the papers once more for the size of our boney.

The sound of a band playing The Billy Boys.

In the pub, the band are practising The Billy Boys above. Fuck sake, Yolanda's already telling everyone King Billy was gay or at least bi. Funny enough, they seem pretty cool with it.

See our bonefires? Davey Weir tells her, they were lit all along the coast to guide King William's ships. See? he says, pointing to the mural across the road. There's our King Billy on his white charger.

Oh, yeah, says Yolanda, you know his horse was called Sorrel?

Oh aye, says Davey the bluffer, Sorrel, that's him.

Well, William confiscated him from the Jacobites, but Sorrel had the last laugh because he bucked him off and he died of his injuries a few days later. Imagine, a Catholic horse killed King Billy!

And she's having a right oul giraffe and Davey Weir is ripping with rage, takes a right reddener, looking like he'd kill us, and me trying to keep me face straight.

King Billy was also a sexist, Davey. His wife Mary was going to be crowned Queen of England but he insisted on being king too just to take the power off her.

Here, King William was no sexist – sure he let her reign while he was away at war!

Davey's fit to be tied, but just then, the nine ninety niners, the peelers, wheel round the boney for a wee scout, a wee nosey, and out we go to give them the eye.

Me and Yolanda take a wee gallop round Belfast, round the city centre. It's all churches and pubs, she says, and an idea's coming into my mind. I'm only dancing round it for now but I'd like to stay here and go for me blue badge, no, not a blue badge for a fucking disabled car, a blue badge to be a tourist guide. And not just do tours of the East but the whole city.

The thing is my name's Aaron Orr – my ancestor was a United Irishman who got hung in Carrickfergus. Of course, Carrick's so boring, you'd want to top yourself. But it means Catholics love me for my name and that's why I was picked for the cross-community job. Republican blood beats in here. Orange heart, green blood. And I'm all for a thirty-two county state. No, I am. A thirty-two county Northern Ireland would be great!

I hear there's youth work going and, before I know it, I have an interview. I ask Yolanda if she'll move here with me, but she has to go back for her studies.

As soon as you're done, come back. Sure you could even work in health and safety.

I don't know, Aaron.

And she says something for the first time. A Dutch quote she's never mentioned before. 'Two religions on one pillow; there lies the devil in between,' and I know she's feeling it. Davey Weir looking at her like she doesn't belong.

But it'll be grand, I say. People are open now.

You see the world through rose-tinted tentacles, Aaron

– and I haven't the heart to correct her. But the thing is ... I love her.

And I see it. Just on me periph. A meat wagon. A convoy of white vans. It's like a balloon's burst in my chest.

Oh, shit! The contractors are on a raid. There's no one at the boney to stop them.

The vans scream to a halt, the men in black, in balaclavas pile out.

I'll stop them, says Yolanda and she starts climbing the pallets.

And what can I do but clamber after her, her taking the lead, and we're soon up on the boards, the riot squad in their baggie blues around us, helmeted and batoned like Robocops. FFFFF of static like we're on top of the moon.

You are trespassing on council property. If you don't come down willingly, you will be arrested.

Houston, are you reading us? I shout back at the arseholes. You are trespassing on the people's property!

And we've no scarves, no hoods, it's not us that are hiding our identities, it's them who act like they're against the law. No registration numbers on the contractor's vans, no faces, no names, just numbers on the peelers' riot suits.

People are racing out their houses, running over to watch Yolanda and me. And Deano breaks through the peeler line, and Dairy Lea and even Davey Weir pushes through, but the peelers are going wild and it's bang with their batons like they're flaying a drum, skulls breaking, folk freaking, more fucking blood than a butcher's apron, and we're still on the boney and soon Bethany and her crew and the kids and the youngbloods are shielding us, and Jamesie leaps up and shouts *Tuaisceart Erin go Bragh*!

Wind your neck in, says Davey Weir, but Yolanda starts shouting it and she's one of us now, and *Tuaisceart Erin go Bragh* we all shout, Northern Ireland forever!

Tuaisceart Erin go Bragh!

Rush of drums.

KING WILLIAM III: We outflanked them in the morning mist, our muskets were too strong for the Irish scythes and swords, but just then the Jacobite cavalry came back at us, driving us into the Boyne, and Schomberg was wounded. I watched him die in the water, the river foamed red with it. James was winning, the battle was almost his, but the coward gave the order to retreat, his forces scattered and that was the end of them. Our scouts say his Irishmen are so angry they've renamed him *Séamus a Chacha* – Seamus the Shit.

And look, up there, from hill to hill, the fires are starting to spread the message that the House of Orange has won and we are on the march to Dublin and the future is ours.

And so, soldiers, let us race on under our Orange banners. From this day on, let fire be the sign of my victory and let orange flame proclaim that both England and Ireland are joined for ever.

Acknowledgements

Thanks to the Arts Council of Northern Ireland, to Rab, and to all those who helped take this show to Edinburgh. And thanks to everyone I've ever got blitzed with at a Belfast boney.

About the Author

Rosemary Jenkinson is a playwright and short story writer from Belfast. She taught English in Greece, France, the Czech Republic and Poland before returning to Belfast in 2002. Plays include *The Bonefire* (Stewart Parker BBC Radio Award), *White Star of the North, Planet Belfast, Here Comes the Night, Michelle and Arlene, May the Road Rise Up* and *Lives in Translation*. Her plays have been performed in Dublin, London, Edinburgh, Brussels, Melbourne, New York and Washington DC. She was artist-in-residence at the Lyric Theatre Belfast and the Leuven Centre for Irish Studies. In 2018 she received a Major Artist Award from the Arts Council of Northern Ireland.

Short story collections include *Contemporary Problems Nos. 53 & 54, Aphrodite's Kiss, Catholic Boy* (shortlisted for the EU Prize for Literature) and *Lifestyle Choice 10mgs* (shortlisted for the Edge Hill Prize). She was singled out by the *Irish Times* for 'an elegant wit, terrific characterisation and an absolute sense of her own particular Belfast'.

Her latest collection, *Marching Season,* is published by Arlen House, and distributed internationally by Syracuse University Press.